Creative Ideas Transfers to Paint

Dozens of **creative** transfer designs offer countless **possibilities** for adding a painter's touch to your home décor and wardrobe. The designs are also perfect for making special **gifts** that your family and **friends** will love. Our gallery of projects provides inspiration for the many ways to create using these **versatile** designs. The projects are painted with acrylic paints and paint markers on fabric and **wood surfaces**, but you can enjoy using the line art motifs for **embroidery**, paper crafting, wood burning, leather crafting, and much more. Use your **imagination** and enlarge or reduce the designs as you decorate everything from casual totes to elegant pillows, from small **handbags** to large **furniture** pieces. Paint T-shirts and greeting cards with holiday designs, then adorn your jeans with colorful butterflies and flowers for a smashing fashion statement. Fanciful dragons, **cute** ghosts, and **adorable** kittens are sure to delight the children in your life. With something for every style and season, this book will definitely become a favorite resource for your **painting** projects.

Contents

General Instructions

There are numerous ways to use the creative designs in this book. You can iron them directly onto almost any fabric or heavy paper. The permanent iron-ons will usually transfer up to three times. You can also use traditional transferring methods to apply the designs to wood, tin, leather, and more. Enlarge and reduce them on a copy machine to customize the designs to fit your needs. Follow the instructions below for easy transferring and painting using whichever method you choose.

transferring on fabric and paper

Included in the book are small test transfers. Use them on a scrap of fabric or paper similar to your project to help you determine the best iron temperature and length of time needed to achieve a good transfer. **Note:** *Before you start your project make sure not to include the test transfer and page number in your design.* The printed transfer is permanent after it is heat-set, so be sure to follow the steps below before transferring your design to clothing, fabric, or paper.

1. If you are transferring a design to a fabric item that will be washed, first wash and dry the item without using fabric softener; press.
2. Preheat the iron for five minutes on appropriate setting for item being used. **Do not** use steam.
3. Because transfer ink may bleed through fabric, protect ironing surface with a clean piece of scrap fabric or paper.
4. Place transfer **inked side down** on the **right side** of fabric or paper. For fabric projects, pin around outside of design to hold in place. Cover the design area with a piece of tissue paper. Place your hot iron on top of transfer; hold for 10-15 seconds (or time determined with your test pattern). **Do not** slide iron. Lift straight up and down and apply even pressure. For large transfers, pick up iron and move to another position until you've applied the entire

design. Carefully lift one corner of transfer to see if design has been transferred to item. If not, place the iron on the transfer for a few more seconds.

alternative transferring method

Transfers may not show up on dark fabrics, but you can easily transfer the designs using white or light colored dressmaker's tracing paper.

1. Pull fabric taut over a piece of cardboard covered with plastic to provide a smooth area for transferring and for later protecting your work surface from any paint that may soak through the fabric.
2. Trace the design onto transparent tracing paper. Flip design for the correct orientation and place on fabric in desired position.
3. Slip the dressmaker's tracing paper, coated side down, between the traced design and the fabric; tape or pin design and fabric to hold in place. Use a tracing wheel, stylus, or dull pencil to draw over design lines.

painting on fabric

1. If painting on an item that will not be washed, use water-based acrylic paint and thin with water. If item will be washed, test for colorfastness before beginning. Use fabric paint or a mixture of half textile medium and half acrylic paint.
2. Be sure the surface beneath the painted area is protected from paint that may soak through fabric.
3. Designs can be shaded or highlighted to add dimension to the project. To shade an area, dampen brush with water then blot on a paper towel. Dip one corner of brush into a paint darker than the base coated area. Stroke brush on a palette a few times to blend. Apply paint along outline area using a continuous smooth stroke. For highlighting use a color that's lighter than the color beneath it.
4. Add outlines and detail lines using a fine-point permanent pen or liner paintbrush and paint.

5. Cover all transfer lines completely. After painting has dried, follow paint manufacturer's instructions to heat-set and launder.

6. Fabric markers are a good alternative for some designs. Test markers on a scrap of fabric. When coloring adjacent areas of a design, allow each color to dry before adding next color. Follow manufacturer's instructions for drying time and heat-setting, if needed.

transferring on wood and tin

1. Prepare your wood or tin surface as follows:
   Wood Surfaces: Fill any holes or dents with wood filler. Sand the entire piece with medium-grit sandpaper and remove any dust. Apply a coat of wood sealer and allow to dry thoroughly. Sand again with fine-grit sandpaper and wipe clean.
   Tin/Metal Surfaces: For pre-finished tin, rinse with a mix of white vinegar + water (1:1) to remove any oil or residue, then it's ready to paint. For used or unfinished tin, first remove any rust using naval jelly. Wash thoroughly with soap and water and allow to dry completely, then rinse with the vinegar and water mix as instructed above. Sand the entire piece with fine-grit sandpaper and remove any dust. Apply a coat of primer or a thin coat of matte spray and let dry.

2. Apply an overall background color to the surface using water-based acrylic paints. Keep the surface as smooth and even as possible by painting with a large brush and applying several light coats rather than a single heavy one. Always let the paint dry between coats.

3. Trace the design onto transparent tracing paper. Flip tracing over for correct orientation and tape to surface in desired position. Slip a piece of transfer or graphite paper underneath the tracing with colored side down. Use gray paper for projects with light backgrounds and white paper for projects with dark backgrounds.

4. Trace over the design using a pencil, inkless pen, or small end of a stylus.

painting on wood and tin

1. Paint with water-based bottled acrylic paints. You may also use acrylic enamels for painting tin projects.

2. For shading, highlighting, and detailing instructions, refer to steps 3 and 4 for painting on fabric.

3. When paint is dry, remove any visible transfer lines using a white art eraser.

4. Apply one or more coats of water-based varnish to protect the painted surface.

painting with markers

Paint the brushless way using fast-drying, permanent paint markers. Here are some tips to get you started.

1. Let dry thoroughly before putting one color on top of another. Colors will blend slightly if not completely dry. Use this to your advantage for shading.

2. Clean tips with baby wipes, if needed.

3. Store with the tip facing downward.

4. Protect your painted design by applying one or more coats of water-based varnish.

adding embroidered accents to your painting

Add extra dimension to your painted designs by embellishing with embroidery (see page 5). Suggested uses for stitches include: Backstitches, Running Stitches, or Stem Stitches for lettering, outlining, and flower stems; Satin Stitches when a solid look is desired for berries, small leaves, and flower petals; French Knots for flower centers, small berries, and eyes; Lazy Daisy Stitches for small flower petals and leaves; Straight Stitches to add detail lines to small areas.

1. Before stitching with dark floss on light fabric, you may wish to set the floss color by soaking floss in a mixture of 1 tablespoon vinegar and 8 ounces of water. Allow floss to air dry.

2. For most embroidery, we recommend using 3 strands of floss. Use 2 strands for a more delicate look or 4 strands for heavier coverage. Cut floss into 18" lengths. Floss this length does not fray or tangle as easily as longer lengths.

3. Because the transfer ink is permanent, be sure stitches cover all transfer lines.

backstitch

Come up at 1, go down at 2, and come up at 3 . Continue working as shown. Length of stitches may be varied as desired.

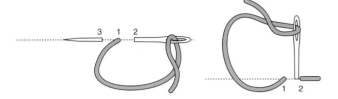

french knot

Come up at 1. Wrap thread twice around needle and insert needle at 2, holding end of thread with non-stitching fingers. Tighten knot; then pull needle through, holding floss until it must be released. For larger knot, use more strands; wrap only once.

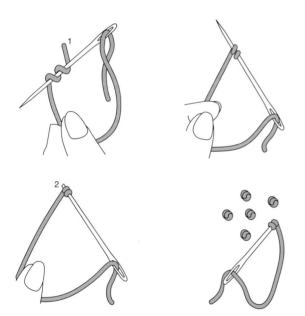

lazy daisy stitch

Bring needle up at 1; take needle down again at 1 but not in the same hole to form a loop; bring needle up at 2. Keeping loop below point of needle, take needle down at 3 to anchor loop.

 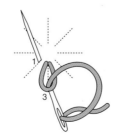

running stitch

The running stitch consists of a series of straight stitches with the stitch length equal to the space between stitches.

satin stitch

Come up at 1. Go down at 2, and come up at 3. Continue until area is filled.

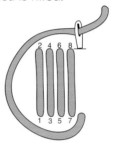

stem stitch

Come up at 1. Keeping thread below stitching line, go down at 2 and come up at 3. Go down at 4 and come up at 5.

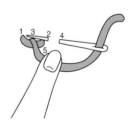

straight stitch

Bring needle up at 1 and take needle down at 2. Length of stitches may be varied as desired.

Gallery

test pattern

8

test pattern

10

AWAKEN EACH
MORNING
WITH JOY

HE WHO PLANTS
KINDNESS
GATHERS LOVE

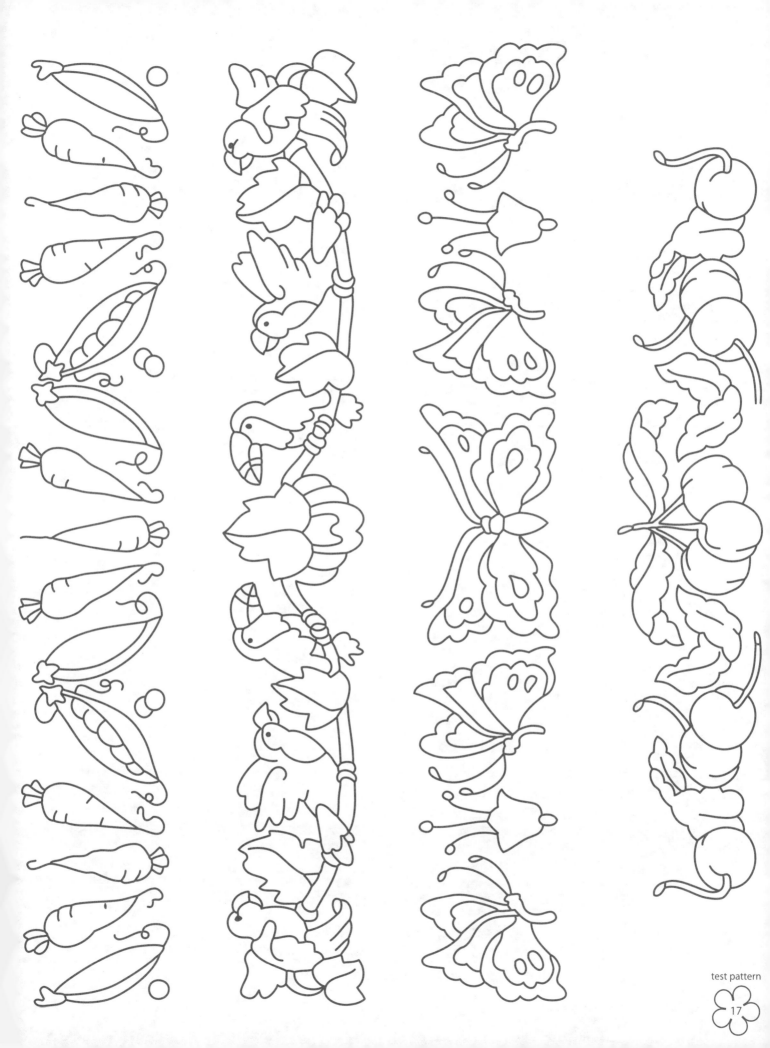

test pattern

17

test pattern

23

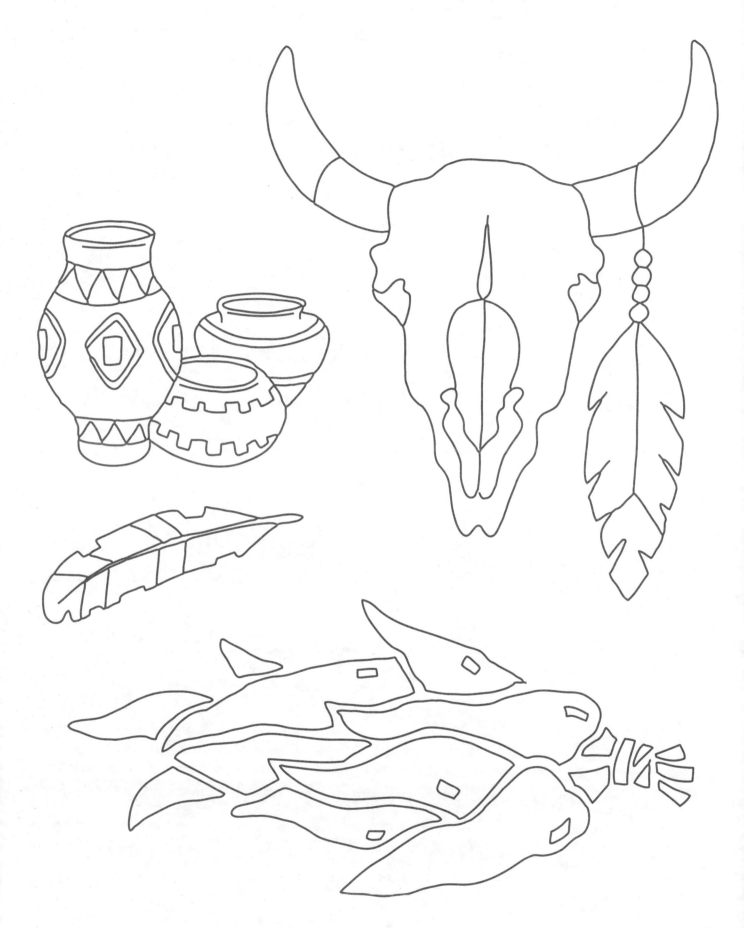

test pattern

26

test pattern

27

test pattern

test pattern

29

test pattern

32

test pattern

34

test pattern

35

WELCOME

I ♥ SNOW

test pattern

37

test pattern

41

WHILE THE POT BOILS

FRIENDSHIP BLOSSOMS

WHILE THE POT BOILS

FRIENDSHIP BLOSSOMS

I
HE WHO PLANTS
KINDNESS
GATHERS LOVE

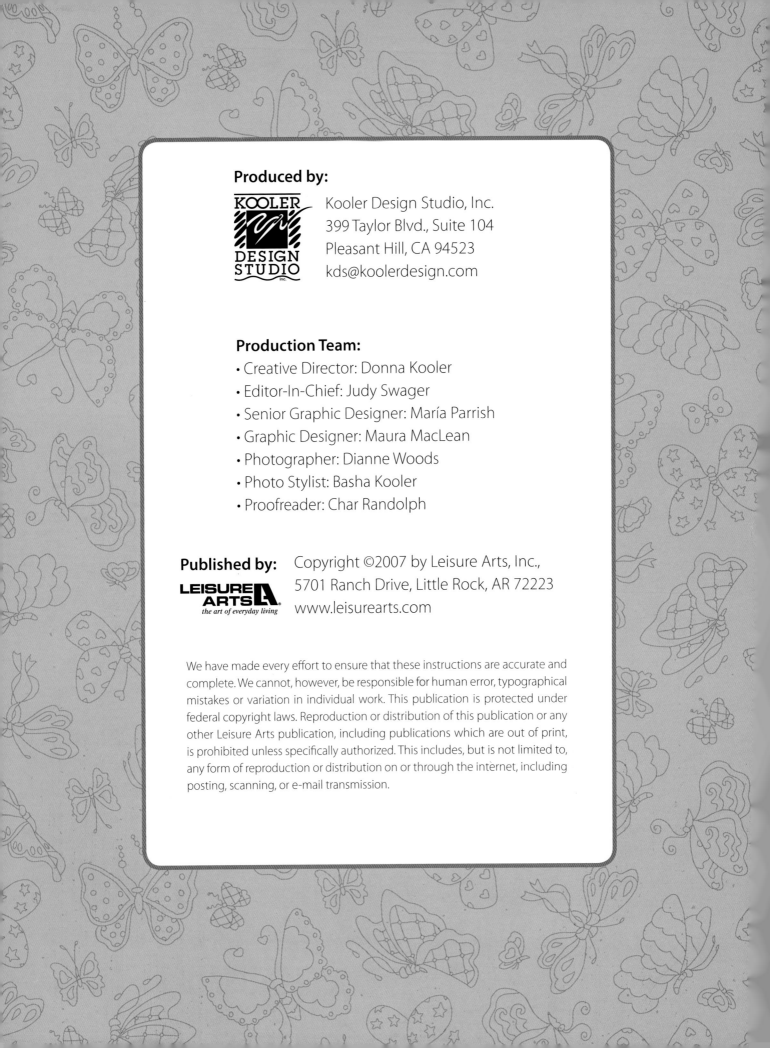

Produced by:

Kooler Design Studio, Inc.
399 Taylor Blvd., Suite 104
Pleasant Hill, CA 94523
kds@koolerdesign.com

Production Team:
• Creative Director: Donna Kooler
• Editor-In-Chief: Judy Swager
• Senior Graphic Designer: María Parrish
• Graphic Designer: Maura MacLean
• Photographer: Dianne Woods
• Photo Stylist: Basha Kooler
• Proofreader: Char Randolph

Published by:

Copyright ©2007 by Leisure Arts, Inc.,
5701 Ranch Drive, Little Rock, AR 72223
www.leisurearts.com